Speed Reading How to Triple Your Reading Speed in Less Than 12 Hours

Stefan Anderson

TO ALL OF THOSE WHO SEEK TO READ MORE

Table of Contents

Introduction

Welcome to the 2nd edition of Speed Reading! New content for those that are experienced with speed reading as well as exercises.

Whether stories took the form of pictures carved onto flat rock surfaces, a series of symbols scratched onto thin pieces of papyrus, or a universal set of 26 symbols called the alphabet typed onto a computer, mankind has always read. We oftentimes don't consider its origin or acknowledge just how vital it is to our success as humans, but reading is something almost all of us do every day. (In fact, you're doing it right now.) It's been around since man first learned to communicate, and, not surprisingly, it's continued to serve a vital role throughout history. Our ability to read has allowed Emperor Hirohito to announce Japan's unconditional surrender in 1945, John F. Kennedy to broadcast "The Decision to go to the Moon" in 1961, and Martin Luther King Jr. to recite his famous "I have a dream speech" in 1963.

In recent years, however, a new form of reading has emerged. It still requires our ability to interpret the combination of our 26 letters into meaningful words, sentences, paragraphs, and ideas, but it involves the employment of a different region of our brain. This form of reading is known as speed reading. And much like its name suggest, the crux of speed reading rests upon our ability to recognize and comprehend words and sentences at a rate much faster than regular reading. And in a society that hinges upon the obsession with speed and fast results, it makes sense that speed reading has rooted itself in our approach to reading.

But regardless of speed reading's universal revitalization in recent years, our ability to speed read is not universal. First and foremost, your speed reading potential depends on your cognitive abilities.

For example, the average college-level reader will generally find that their speed reading success is better than a middle school-level reader. This stems, in part, from the college-level reader's larger vocabulary and their experience with reading difficult texts with broader topics. However, this doesn't mean you need a college degree to be a successful speed reader. Actually, with enough practice, anyone can increase their reading speed. Like everything else we do, it takes practice, time, patience, dedication, and motivation.

Although speed reading seems like a fairly simple process—some may assume you simply read faster than normal—it's actually quite a complex one. Aside from learning to harness the high-functioning power of a different part of your brain, as we'll see in Chapter 3, speed reading requires the application of a multitude of reading techniques and an avoidance of habits our early reading years have taught us. We'll discuss these methods and cautions in further detail later in Chapter 4 and 5, but these techniques can range from processes known as "chunking," taking advantage of your peripheral version, and avoiding the tendency to read linearly and regressively. Perhaps the hardest part about the speed reading process, however, is our need to relearn how to read—whereas our childhood reading instruction taught us to "hear" words as we read them, speed reading requires us to quiet the "hearing" of words and focus on their visual appearance.

If you're beginning to feel a bit overwhelmed or lost, don't fret. Speed reading is certainly a complex process, but we've carefully dedicated each chapter of this book to a single speed reading-related topic to prevent such feelings. Chapter 1 and 2 provide an outline of reading and speed reading, respectively. We've included an introduction to normal reading so that you can better understand the difference between the two reading types. Once you've familiarized with the basics of speed reading, Chapter 3 will then introduce you to the physiological processes in our brain as we speed read. Knowing how your brains function for both reading and speed reading will help as you learn to use the visual region of your brain instead of the auditory. Chapter 4 is where the real fun begins. We've provided three of the most important, effective, and proven speed reading techniques that'll help you increase your reading rates (the words you're able to read per minute, also known as "wmp"). Once you have these techniques in mind, Chapter 5 will introduce the reading habits you should avoid as you speed read and Chapter 6 will help you set up a conducive speed reading environment in which you can practice the techniques you've learned in Chapters 4 and 5. Chapters 7 and 8 are all about practicing and refining your skills. There'll be speed reading tips, examples, and varying texts that you can practice your speed reading skills on. You'll also find that each text presents a varying and increasing difficulty level—we've done this so that you can go back and practice more once you've progressed from a beginner speed reader to an intermediate speed reader, and from an intermediate speed reader to an expert speed reader. Once you've tackled one or two of these exercises over time, Chapter 9 will then introduce another speed reading technique called speed skimming. If you'd like to learn more about speed reading, are interested in finding a recommended speed reading course, or simply want to practice your speed reading skills on your own, Chapter 11 is the chapter for you.

Chapter 1—Reading Basics

If you want to become a professional football player, you first need to learn the basic rules of the game, right? If you aspire to become the next Michelangelo and paint a chapel ceiling, you first need to complete a painting on a small canvas, correct? Well, learning how to speed read is just like learning the rules of football before you play or refining your painting skills on a canvas before you paint a historic chapel. In order to speed read, we first need to understand how we read.

What is reading?

Reading is when we look at a series of written symbols and derive meaning from them. Our symbols today take the form of the alphabet, but ancient cultures once used picture-orientated symbols as a means to record information or stories. However, the symbols we derive meaning from are not simply limited to the alphabet. Our symbols also come in the form of punctuation

Reading Myth #1: We need to read every word in order.

marks, which tell us when to stop or pause in our reading, and in spaces, which divide words and ideas. Our processing of these written symbols can be silent (when we read in our heads) or aloud (when others can hear us).

The reading process

If we take the thinking and comprehension process out of reading, we're left with a mechanical process that simply involves looking at a word or words. This specific process is known as "**fixation.**" Once an individual is done looking at or fixating on a word (which, by the way, takes the average person an estimated .25 seconds), they move on to the next word and repeat the .25 second fixation process. And if you thought the .25 second fixation process was fast, you'll be interested to know that the "**saccade,**" the mechanical movement of looking from one word to the next, takes an impressive average of .1 second. However, we tend to slow the reading process

Reading Fact #1: No, we don't necessarily need to read word-for-word. Many of the words we encounter as we read are "fluff" words—they're small, undescriptive words that simply build up to the important details or ideas of the text. We don't miss much if we skip these.

done when we take moments out of our reading to pause and find meaning in sentences or comprehend words. But despite our slowing down of the process, these pauses generally consume only .3 to .5 seconds of our time. In short, reading without applying complex thought or comprehension is an extremely quick process. If we add the time spent fixating, saccading, and pausing for comprehension, the average college-level reader reads, on average, an estimated 200 to 400 words per minute.

Now let's add the thinking and comprehension process of reading back into the equation. When we read normally, we interpret the words or text in front of us using our visual thinking processes, which means we see a word or group of words as visual pictures. We also "hear" the text in our head as we read. This is a strange phenomenon to describe, so if you're not sure what we mean when we say this, try it for yourself. Read the following sentences and take note of what happens as you read it:

Read this sentence to yourself. Read it silently and make sure not to move your mouth as you read it. NOW SCREAM THIS SENTENCE AS LOUD AS YOU CAN IN YOUR HEAD! Now whisper this next part in your best British accent. Brilliant, isn't it?

Does our explanation of "hearing" the text inside your head as you read make sense now? It's strange, but so very fascinating. Nonetheless, most people when they read automatically sound the words out in their mind without moving their lips. Unfortunately for those hoping to increase their reading speed, this process causes us to become dependent on hearing the sound of the word in our mind in order for our brains to process it and comprehend. This slows our reading process down significantly.

How we learn to read as children

Before we learn to read as children, the letters on paper are meaningless—we don't know what sound the letter "a" makes, and we don't know what sound the combination of "th" makes. So before we're able to pick up a Dr. Seuss book and comprehend the combination of letters on the page, we first need to learn the relationship between the 26 letters of the alphabet and about 44 **phonemes**, units of sound that distinguish one word from another (pa**d** and pa**t**, or ba**d** and ba**t**, for example).

In addition to memorizing sounds, reading instruction for children also emphasize the "hearing" of sounds. The logic behind this approach is this: If children aren't able to "hear" the *at* sound in *cat* and *bat,* for example, and they don't understand that the difference between "cat" and bat" lies in the first letter of each word, then they'll have a difficult time "sounding out" words at a quick pace and in a smooth fashion. In other words, beginner readers are encouraged and even required to "hear" the sounds they both read and speak aloud. But as we'll see later in Chapter 6, the reading process we are taught as children is the very process that hinders us from becoming effective speed readers.

Chapter 2—Speed Reading Basics

If you're making a multi-layer wedding cake, do you put the biggest cake on the bottom or the top? The answer is the bottom, of course (unless you've figured out a way to defy physics). The relationship between reading and speed reading is like the levels of a wedding cake. Speed reading is a sub-category that falls under the category of reading—it's smaller than the broad category of reading and should therefore be learned after we understand reading, just like the smaller layer of the wedding cake should be put on after we've added the bigger, bottom layer. This is why we've spent some time talking about the normal reading process in Chapter 1 before we began our discussion of speed reading in this chapter and the following chapters. Without reading, we'd have nothing to compare speed reading to.

So now that we've familiarized ourselves with the reading process, we can begin to learn about the basics of speed reading.

Reading Myth #2:
Accelerated reading reduces comprehension.

What is speed reading?

Speed reading is when we read rapidly by grouping words, phrases, or sentences. Whereas the average reader registers and reads 200 to 400 words per minute, the average speed reader can register and read an estimated 1,000 to 1,700 words per minute, though greater word per minute rates have also been recorded.

How do reading and speed reading differ?

In Chapter 1, we briefly discussed how the mechanical reading process involves fixation, saccade, and brief pauses for comprehension. Although it also includes these processes, speed reading shortens the amount of time spent on each mechanical reading process. We'll discuss speed reading's techniques in more detail later in Chapter 4, but it should be noted here that speed reading differs from regular reading because it drastically cuts down on time spent reading by chunking words and sentences together, taking advantage of our peripheral vision, and employing sub-vocalization techniques. Whereas mechanical reading is a natural process, speed reading, with its goal of registering words in less than .25 seconds, is an artificial but somewhat efficient reading process.

How programs teach speed reading

Programs designed to teach and enhance speed reading skills will start with speed-building exercises. These training and practice exercises will focus on accelerating your reading speed by eliminating the habit of mentally sounding out the written texts as you read them. Again, this process will be further explored later in Chapter 6 when we discuss sub-vocalization.

Once you've completed your speed-building exercises, the course's training will typically shift to re-teaching you how to read. The main objective behind this approach is to displace the deep-rooted reading habits that we develop in our early years of reading with a more effective and sophisticated reading and thinking habit. This step in the speed reading learning process is crucial—without a more sophisticated reading and thought process, our speed reading comprehension would be rendered useless.

A brief history of speed reading

Evelyn Nielsen Wood first introduced speed reading in 1957 after her observation that sweeping her finger across the page while reading resulted in an increased reading rate. Many of the speed reading techniques we use today are linked to Wood's initial observations, and her dedication to the speed reading process shows through her ability to read far faster than the average person—Wood's reading comprehension averages to be a shocking 2,700 words per minute. Moreover, Wood's speed reading principles have become the cornerstone of today's speed reading

Reading Fact #2: Our ability to comprehend the materials we speed read depends on how well we can extract and retain the information. Speed reading techniques like "chunking" help us read faster, but it also ensures we've comprehended the important details or concepts of the text, for example.

process and techniques, and because of such, these fundamentals have become known as the Evelyn Wood Reading Dynamics.

Following Wood's discovery of this previously untapped skill, many speed reading programs began to pop up with the sole intent of teaching students to read at accelerated rates. Despite speed reading's waned popularity in the 1990s, recent years have seen a revival in mastering the speed reading skill, especially in the app and course-offering industries which have reintroduced the skill of speed reading and have revitalized the public's interest.

Fun Fact:

Much like we don't need to read every word in a text, we also don't need to read every letter of a word. Interesting, huh? As long as the first and last letter of the word remains the same, our brains are able to decode and comprehend the words in a text without reading the word's individual letters. This is because our brains are more concerned with understanding the meaning of a word rather than a word's exact letter placement. Take a look at the following passage and see for yourself:

Aoccdrnig to rseearch at Cmarbigde Uinervity, it deosn't mttaer in waht oredr the ltteers in a wrod are, the olny iprmotnat tihng is taht the fsirt and lsat ltteer be in hte rghit pclae.

Tihs is bcuseae the haumn mnid deosn't raed eervy ltteer by istelf, but the wrod as a wohle.

Chapter 3—How Speed Reading Works

Speed reading is certainly a complex process, but rest assured—the techniques we'll discuss in Chapter 4, 5, and 6 will make learning and practicing speed reading a much simpler, enjoyable, and beneficial process. The actual science behind how our brains work when we read and speed read is a complex but fascinating process, too. But again, we've tried to explain the science behind reading in a way that makes sense to everyone. After all, knowing what's going on inside your mind as you speed read is a great way to reduce those feelings of intimidation or to better understand the speed reading process. Understanding the difference between your visual cortex and auditory cortex, for example, might seem irrelevant, especially for those uninterested in science. However, knowing how these two active regions of your brain function as you read may actually help you later in the speed reading process when you need to quiet your auditory cortex and harness the power of your visual cortex.

Your brain and speed reading

Speed reading is all about the **visual cortex,** the region of our brain designated to rapidly processing everything we see throughout our day. It's riddled with neurons, which means it functions and processes visuals faster than other parts of the brain that contain lower volumes of neurons. As we delve into how our brain processes reading and speed reading, however, it's important to note that one of the regions of the brain with less neurons than the visual cortex is the **auditory**

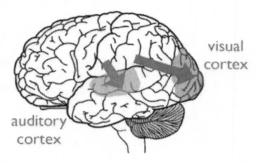

cortex. While the visual cortex plays a crucial role in our ability to speed read, the auditory cortex plays an important role in our ability to read normally. Recall earlier in Chapter 1 when we discussed how we learn to read by "hearing" sounds. Our auditory cortex, which passes the sounds we hear into our cortex for interpretation, allows us to "hear" the difference between cat, bat, and fat. It plays a vital role as we learn to read by memorizing the sounds letters and phenomes make. But as we've started to discuss, "hearing" words is a slower reading process than "seeing" the words. It follows, then, that using our auditory cortex when we read creates a slower reading process than using our visual cortex. So when we're able to harness the power of our rapidly-functioning visual cortex, we can accomplish more things in less time, especially when it comes to speed reading.

You'll find that most speed reading training programs develop speed reading skills by harnessing the power of the visual cortex. These programs help us deal with or limit our instinctive use of "mentally" speaking and hearing the words when we read. When these programs teach us to stop our internal voicing of words as we read them, they teach us to reduce our use of the auditory cortex and encourage the activation of our visual cortex. With enough speed reading practice, the visual cortex should become the dominant text-processing region of our brain—we'll no longer "hear" words; we'll "see" them. Because the visual cortex sees text as images, speed reading becomes a similar process to the ones we use when we look at picture books or watch a movie.

Effectiveness of speed reading

If we base the effectiveness of speed reading off of how many words we can read per minute, it's a highly effective process. However, academics and researchers have voiced their concerns for speed reading in recent publications and studies. They claim, and perhaps rightfully so, that speed reading is not an effective process to employ if our outcome is to improve reading comprehension. If we take some time to reflect on such statements, there certainly is some validity to them. We typically do read with the intention to comprehend and learn. However, speed reading programs limit our ability to comprehend when they frown upon re-reading confusing passages and pausing to ensure we've understood and retained the reading material. When we don't re-read or pause, we lose vital information, which therein limits our comprehension.

This is not to say, however, that speed reading does nothing in terms of comprehension. Some speed readers do show varying levels of text comprehension despite the rapid pace in which they read the material. Academics and researchers suggest that these levels of speed reading comprehension may be a result of a person's familiarity with the subject or text.

So, what does all of this mean exactly? Well, it essentially means that speed reading is a great tool to employ if you:

- Have read the text before and understood it

- Are looking for a particular passage

- Want a brief overview of the passage by reading bullet points, bold, italicized, or underlined words or phrases.

- Are familiar with the topic

Factors of effective speed reading

Because speed reading rates vary so drastically—some readers can read 600 words per minute while others can read 2,000 words per minute—it makes sense that there are several factors that play a role in our ability to speed read and our success. Some of the most common factors that affect our speed reading rates include:

- Nature of the material

- Alertness of the reader

- Mental speed of the reader

- Amount of practice

Nature of the material

Some materials are naturally harder to read than others. A child's picture book is far easier to speed read than a PhD dissertation on the comparative analysis of nineteenth-century racial amalgamation and twenty-first-century post-racialist thinking. Complex topics—which are often filled with technical or unfamiliar words—that are geared toward a limited academic audience typically prove difficult for the average speed reader. However, the topic of the reading material is not the only factor that makes a text harder or easier to read and comprehend. The formatting and presentation of a text also plays a crucial role on our ability to understand a text—while convoluted and lengthy paragraphs make a text harder to speed read, the use of bullet points to break up materials or the inclusion of helpful diagrams typically makes a text more accessible.

Alertness of the reader

It's a rather simple factor, but your alertness can play a major part in your ability to speed read material. When we fail to give speed reading our undivided attention, we often fail to absorb important concepts and we lower our comprehension rates. When this happens, we tend to re-read what has already been read, which naturally slows our reading rate.

Mental speed of the reader

Again, it's a rather basic factor, but it's an important one nonetheless. Our cognitive ability and our reading level influence how we read and how fast we read. A college-level speed reader, for example, has a much better chance of achieving a higher speed reading rate than an elementary student who is learning to write in complete sentences.

Amount of practice

Like everything else we pursue, speed reading requires practice. It's not a natural skill, so it's important that we dedicate time to practicing and refining our speed reading methods and skills. What's great about this book is that we've included multiple practice materials that you can try once you've familiarized yourself with the effective and proven speed reading techniques, have learned about the things successful speed readers avoid when they read, and have set up your speed reading environment. These practice materials, along with additional materials that you can use to assess your work and progress, can be found in Chapter 8.

Chapter 4—Speed Reading Techniques

Much of what we've discussed so far has revolved around familiarizing ourselves with the reading and speed reading process, whether it's been learning about how our brain works when we speed read or learning about how effective experts suggest speed reading really is (which, by the way, it is—that is, it is if we're looking to read a large amount of words in a short amount of time and we're okay with sacrificing a bit of text-comprehension in the process).

But with all that reading background and speed reading fundamental talk aside, we can finally dive into the fun topics of speed reading, which we're sure you've been dying to read. So without further ado, this chapter is dedicated to explaining and exemplifying the three most effective and success-proven techniques of speed reading.

Chunking

Remember in Chapter 1 when we talked about the mechanical process of reading? (We spend about .25 seconds on fixation, .1 second on saccade, and .4 seconds on comprehension pauses.) Well, the method of chunking words—reading multiple words as one whole unit—is all about cutting down those seconds and ensuring that our increased reading hasn't resulted in decreased comprehension. Chunking is so highly praised because it discourages fixation on individual words—when we concentrate on each word we read, we have the tendency to miss overarching themes or important details. It's also a speed reading favorite because it helps us read fast while also keeping track of important information we come across.

Some have compared the technique of chunking to eating rice—much like eating rice by the spoonful rather than by the grain allows you to eat more and save time, reading words in chunks rather than individually lets us read more in a shorter period of time, too.

Specifically, chunking is when we combine multiple words into a single thought. So, instead of reading the following passage like normal,

Herman Melville is a canonical nineteenth-century author whose publication list is quite diverse. From his novel *Typee* to *Moby-Dick*, Melville's novels often take place on or around the sea and include critical commentaries pertaining to the racial or cultural Other,

chunking would have us read the passage like this:

Herman Melville | canonical nineteenth-century | *Typee Moby-Dick* | on or around the sea | critical commentaries | racial or cultural other.

Essentially, we ignore the "fluff" of the passage as we read—the unhelpful little words that don't say much—and hone in on the important details like who Melville was, what he wrote, and the common themes of his book. Ignoring the unimportant parts and, instead, focusing on the crucial *Who, What, Where, When, Why, and How* of the text will help you read through the material faster while still comprehending what is read.

This method can be slightly confusing when we're first beginning to learn it, however. There's a common misconception that chunking simply means pairing every two words of a sentence. (Theboy wentto thestore toget themilk). This isn't entirely accurate. Yes, we've chunked words together in this example, but it doesn't do much in terms of increasing our reading speed or helping us retain information.

> Chunking involves the pulling of grouped words that, when we look at them separately from the text, give us a fairly detailed idea of what the text was about.

Instead, chunking involves the pulling of grouped words that, when we look at them separately from the text, give us a fairly detailed idea of what the text was about. Still confused? That's alright. Check out the following sections that discuss specific chunking techniques and show examples of exactly what we mean.

Skim Chunking

Like we've discussed, chunking is when we combine multiple words as one whole unit when we read. But there's also another important component of chunking that we haven't yet discussed. This component of chunking is called **skimming,** which is when we quickly read over the words we see without focusing on each individual word. So, if you think you've got a handle on how chunking works, you're ready to see how chunking with skimming can be applied as we speed read.

Let's say that you're speed reading the following paragraph using skim chunking:

Edgar Allan Poe is a nineteenth-century American author who was born in Boston, Massachusetts on January 19, 1809. Although Poe is best known for his tales of mystery and the macabre, which often take the form of poetry and short stories, he is also the author of a racially-charged novel called *The Narrative of Arthur Gordon Pym of Nantucket*. This novel, however, is far less popular than his other works of poetry and fiction such as "The Black Cat," "The Tell-Tale Heart," and "The Raven."

Using the skim chunking method, your reading of the paragraph should look something like this:

Edgar Allan Poe is a nineteenth-century **American author** who was born in **Boston,** Massachusetts on January 19, **1809.** Although Poe is best known for his **tales of mystery and the macabre**, which often take the form of **poetry and short stories**, he is also the author of a **racially-charged novel** called

The Narrative of Arthur Gordon Pym of Nantucket. This novel, however, is far less known than his other works of poetry and fiction such as **"The Black Cat, "The Tell-Tale Heart," and "The Raven."**

The bold-faced words in the above paragraph show the important words you should have chunked as you were reading. These words give you a general sense of what the paragraph is saying without having to read every single word. If we remove the bold-faced words, for example, we have:

Chunking is all about combining words to shorten the amount of time we spend reading a text, but it's also about combining the words that best provide an overall summary of the text.

Edgar Allan Poe, American author, Boston, 1809, tales of mystery and the macabre, poetry and short stories, racially-charged novel, "The Black Cat," "The Tell-Tale Heart," and "The Raven."

That gives us a pretty good sense of what the paragraph was about, doesn't it? It also gives us an equally good sense of who Poe was and what he wrote. The best part about this is that we were able to derive meaning from this 85 word passage by focusing on only 28 words.

Additionally, the non-boldfaced words show the words you can simply skim over. Remember, you want to read quickly, but you want to comprehend what you read as well.

Diagonal chunking

Diagonal chunking involves chunking an entire paragraph in one smooth swoop. It sounds complicated, right? It might be at first, but with some practice, it's actually a pretty effective chunking technique. So, instead of moving your eyes from left to right when you read, diagonal chunking requires that you move your eyes in, well, a diagonal direction. First, read the first complete sentence. (The first sentence is usually the topic sentence, which means it tells you exactly what the paragraph is about). Then, read the right side of the first line of text, then the left side of the second line of text. Then, read the right side of the second line, then the left side of the third line, and so on. Make sure you're reading only a few words from each side of the sentence you're looking at. Go ahead and give it a try:

Edgar Allan Poe is a nineteenth-century American author who was born in Boston, Massachusetts on January 19, 1809. Although Poe is best known for his tales of mystery and the macabre, which often take the form of poetry and short stories, he is also the author of a racially-charged novel called *The Narrative of Arthur Gordon Pym of Nantucket*. This novel, however, is far less popular than his other works of poetry and fiction such as "The Black Cat, "The Tell-Tale Heart," and "The Raven."

Were you able to distinguish who this paragraph is about and what specifically he is most commonly known for? If you followed the diagonal chunking technique, you'll have read the underlined words and phrases of the following paragraph:

Edgar Allan Poe is a nineteenth-century American author. He was born in Boston, Massachusetts on January 19, 1809. Although Poe is best known for his tales of mystery and the macabre, which often take the form of poetry and short stories, he is also the author of a racially-charged novel called *The Narrative of Arthur Gordon Pym of Nantucket*. This novel, however, is far less known than his other works of poetry and fiction such as "The Black Cat, "The Tell-Tale Heart," and "The Raven."

Based on the underlined words—the words you should have read as you tried diagonal chunking—you get a really great sense of what the paragraph is about by simply reading the beginning and ending words of each line. You know that the paragraph is about:

- Nineteenth-century American author Edgar Allan Poe

- Poe's birth in Boston

- Poe's tales of mystery

- Poe's poetry and short stories

- His novel called *The Narrative of Arthur Gordon Pym of Nantucket*

- Poe's other works of poetry and fiction such as "The Tell-Tale Heart" and "The Raven."

This technique helps you breeze through paragraphs of writing, but it also allows you to grasp hold of the important ideas in each line of writing.

Readjusting your chunking technique

As you apply these chunking methods to your speed reading, be wary of one potential draw back to this technique. Some academics have voiced their concerns that chunking decreases our ability to recall certain details from a text or that chunking makes referencing a slightly more difficult task. The quick fix for this is to be aware as you practice your speed reading for the first time. When you practice, use either the skim chunking or diagonal chunking method, but set aside a few minutes after you've finished reading for reflection. Consider whether or not you were able to explain, in detail, the important concepts of the material you read. Likewise, recall some important ideas you learned and see if you can find them quickly in the text. Refer to one of the following two options depending on what your answers were. Look at 1.) if you could easily explain details and make quick referrals to the text, or look at 2.) if you struggled to explain details and make quick references to the text.

1.) If both of these came easily, that's great. It would seem chunking is a highly effective speed reading tool for you to incorporate into your speed reading routine. If you feel confident in doing so, you can add a bit more complexity to the process of word chunking—instead of chunking a text by a few words, try chunking a text by phrases or sentences. This will increase your comprehension.

2.) If you struggled to explain the details of the reading material or had a hard time referencing concepts from the text on the spot, then you may need to readjust your approach to chunking. So, for example, let's say that you struggled to comprehend the material when you were chunking words together in groups of 5. Try reducing the amount of words you chunk down to 3. Don't fret if you still struggle with this amount of word chunking. This skill will feel awkward at first and will take some time getting used to. If you've spent some time practicing but chunking is still giving you a headache, you might want to consider another speed reading technique. Finding a different technique is perfectly okay. Some methods will inevitable come easier for some and harder for others.

Peripheral vision

When we read sentences word-by-word, our focus is on the one word that is in the middle of our visual field. This is a rooted habit that comes from our early reading instruction when our teachers told us to keep our eyes on one word at a time. Unfortunately, this habit needs to be broken if we want to improve our reading speed—when our eyes only concentrate on our center line of vision, slowly work their way across the line, and then slowly shift to the line below, we lose a lot of precious reading time.

What we aren't taught in school, however, is that our peripheral vision expands 180 degrees. (For those less inclined in math, that's half of a circle...that's a lot). To make this fact a little more relevant, our 180 degree peripheral vision means that our eyes are able to take in about 1.5 inches worth of writing at one time. In other words, this is the difference between seeing one word at a time and seeing a phrase or complete sentence.

What using your peripheral vision looks like

The normal approach to reading, the one when we focus on a single word in our central line of vision and move our head as we read, might look something like this on paper.

The boy went to the store.

The **boy** went to the store.

The boy **went** to the store.

The boy went **to** the store.

The boy went to **the** store.

The boy went to the **store.**

Did you notice how the bold-faced word attracted your attention? Did you feel like your head was moving as the bold-faced word shifted to the right in each sentence? This is how we were taught to read as children. Unfortunately, it's unconducive to the speed reading process in which we want to take in as many words as we can in as little time as possible.

When you sit down to apply the peripheral reading technique to your speed reading process, be sure to soften and relax your gaze. By relaxing your face and expanding your field of vision, your gaze will shift by area rather than by word. You also won't need to move your head, which will reduce your tendency to focus on whatever word is in your direct line of vision.

Getting used to using peripheral vision

If you find yourself needing some help with this skill, find a text and draw two vertical lines down the left and right side of the page. These vertical lines should cut off the first 2-3 words on the left side of the paper and the last 2-3 words on the right side of the paper. Once you have your paper set up, focus your eyes on the middle of the paper. While you keep your attention on the middle of the paper, simultaneously use your peripheral vision to see the words that fall outside of the vertical line. You'll learn what it feels like to use your peripheral vision when you read, and, as an added bonus, you should feel more comfortable doing so.

Quick Tips

Skim chunking, diagonal chunking, and using peripheral vision while speed reading are three extremely effective techniques every speed reader should master. Unfortunately, these methods can take a bit of time and patience. In other words, they're probably not the most ideal strategies if you're hoping to become a speed reading expert overnight. Actually, no technique will really help you become an expert speed reader overnight—it's a skill that takes dedication and practice. However, there are some helpful speed reading tips that have the potential to at least improve your words per minute rate, some even within 12 hours.

- **Determine your motivation**—Acknowledging why you're reading before you begin to read will help keep you on track. Figuring out your motivation for speed reading will also help you focus on both reading fast and retaining/comprehending the material you read.

- **Be dedicated**—Being dedicated to and interested in the material you're reading will help you maintain your attention to the text. When you do this, you're able to read faster, avoid regression, and comprehend more efficiently.

- **Practice in the morning**—It might seem like a small factor, but studies show that we generally learn more when we read earlier in the day (probably because our hectic schedules haven't gotten the best of us yet).

- **Limit distractions**—We'll talk more about this in Chapter 6, but, your speed reading environment should be one with little to no distractions. This means turning your phone on silent and flipping it over, reducing all background noise, and setting yourself up in a private yet comfortable space. Answering a text or listening to a conversation down the hall will only interrupt your reading flow and force you to re-read the text you weren't paying attention to.

- **Read with a pointer**—Using some sort of pointer as you read encourages your eyes to keep moving forward and discourages them from looking at previously read text. This will be further discussed in the next chapter, but using a pointer is especially helpful if you find you have the tendency to frequently re-read.

- **Take breaks**—Sometimes decreased comprehension happens when read too much, too quick, for too long. Taking short breaks—even 10 minutes at a time—will help refresh your brain and your eyes. Not exhausting your brain is crucial for your speed reading success.

- **Preview your material before reading**—Before you sit down to read a text, flip through the pages. Quickly read chapter titles, subtitles, headings, subheadings, introductions, and conclusions. Studies show that speed reading comprehension increases when readers are familiar with the topics, structure, and organization of the materials they read. If you're reading to gain knowledge on a particular topic, knowing a little about each chapter will help you decide whether reading that chapter is relevant or not.

- **Ignore punctuation**—If you're aware of grammatical rules, you know that you should briefly pause when you see a comma in writing and that you should stop when you see a period. (Check for yourself—did you shortly pause when you saw the comma after "rules" and stop when you saw the period after "period"?) Well, speed reading encourages you to avoid these grammatical tendencies. Avoiding pauses and stops from commas and periods in writing will increase—although only somewhat—your reading speed.

- **Expand your vocabulary**—Expanding your vocabulary will decrease the number of times you need to slow down your reading when you come across an unfamiliar word in a text.

- **Stay still**—Fidgeting or giving in to your habits (like nail biting, hair twirling, or foot stomping) distracts you, to varying degrees, from what you're reading. Sitting still will ensure your only focus is on the reading material in front of you.

Prioritize your reading material by importance—If you plan on reading multiple texts, be sure to establish which ones are the most important and which ones are the least important. Always read the ones that are most important—reading with a clear, fresh mind is an important element of retaining and comprehending information. If it helps, you can sort your reading materials into piles to help keep them organized.

Chapter 5—What to Avoid When Speed Reading

So we spent some time in the last chapter learning about the most effective speed reading techniques (skim chunking, diagonal chunking, and using our peripheral vision) that have been proven to increase our word per minute reading rate, but have also been proven to reduce our loss of comprehension rates as we speed read. If you think you have a steady handle on the previous speed reading techniques, you're now ready to turn your attention to some of the things you should avoid as you speed read.

Regression

Regression has quite a few different meanings, but when we use it in the context of speed reading, **regression** refers to the unnecessary re-reading of a text. Although it's a subtle reading habit, most of us do it. Some of us do it when we daze off for a

Reading Myth #3:
Some people struggle to speed read because their eyes aren't strong enough or simply can't move fast enough.

second and have to re-read the words we just read. Others do it when they start thinking about their to-do list and find that they need to re-read the last couple of sentences, or worse, the last couple of paragraphs. Other times, we simply regress when we want to make sure that we've actually read something right. It's a natural habit, but it's one that takes up our precious reading time because it causes us to lose our flow, which often results in our decreased understanding.

The quick fix

If you find that you're guilty of frequent regression, try running some form of a pointer underneath the lines you read. Your pointer can be anything from a ruler, your finger, or the tip of a pen. When you do this, you should notice that your eyes follow the tip of the pointer, which will help you avoid skipping back to words or sentences previously read. Keep in mind that the speed at which you move the pointer will affect the speed at which you read the text. This is a great technique to reduce regression, but be sure to keep your pointer constantly moving. Stopping and starting your pointer's movement will encourage you to fixate on individual words, which, as we've seen in previous chapters, is highly unconducive to increasing your speed reading rate.

Linear Reading

As you may be beginning to notice, the otherwise helpful habits we were taught in elementary school are all of the habits we need to break if we want to succeed at speed reading. **Linear reading,** which is when we read every word, sentence, paragraph, and page in sequential order—across and down—is no exception. When we read linearly, we spend as much time reading the supplementary (the less important) information as we do with the important information. But speed reading is, in part, about limiting our time spent reading supplementary text and increasing our time spent reading and retaining the important parts of the text. This is why we should avoid reading each and every word we see in order.

Reading Fact #3: If you take advantage of your peripheral vision, which lets you see 180 degrees, you won't need to depend on the movement of your eyes when you speed read.

When we recommend avoiding linear reading, however, we're not advising you to speed read a paragraph starting from the last sentence, jumping to the first sentence, and ending with the middle sentences, of course. You should still approach reading the paragraph like you would normally, but you shouldn't feel pressed to spend time reading each and every word. Instead, the steps of nonlinear reading might look something like this:

1. Read the entire first sentence of each paragraph. The first sentence is generally the topic sentence, which should give you some idea of what the paragraph is about or how it is organized. When you're speed reading, comprehension will come easier if you already have an idea of what the paragraph is discussing.

2. Speed read each paragraph using the skim chunking and diagonal chunking techniques we learned in Chapter 4.

3. While you use these two speed reading technique, use your peripheral vision to take note of any words, sentences, or phrases

that are formatted differently from the rest of the text. For example, look for words or sentences that are:

- **Bolded**

- *Italicized*

- <u>Underlined</u>

- Bulleted

- Numbered (1, 2, 3)

- Asterisked (**)

- *In a different font*

- In a different color

• In a different font size

More often than not, words, sentences, or phrases that are written in a different format than the rest of the text are intended to stick out to the reader. Speed readers should take advantage of this. For example, bolded, italicized, or underlined words are often vocabulary words and bulleted words are often a simple and clear way of listing multiple important concepts or ideas (like we've done above).

You should also skim your reading material for organizational formatting such as:

- Chapter titles

- Subtitles

- Headers

Titles, subtitles, and headers are a broad way of finding exactly what you're looking for when compared to searching for bolded vocabulary words, but they're definitely a good place to start. If you've been given a photocopied handout of chapter 1-10 of a science textbook, for example, and have been asked to learn about photosynthesis, flipping through the chapter titles is a great way to reduce your time spent reading the first couple paragraphs of each chapter. Chapters titled "Human Sexuality" and "Organic Chemistry" won't seem like potential chapters that discuss plants and photosynthesis once you've flipped through the handout and have seen chapters titled "Plants and Animals."

In a similar way, headers typically provide a clear gist of what a section of writing will be about (notice throughout this book, for example, that within each chapter, there are bolded headers that either ask a question that will be answered in the following text, or state an idea that will be discussed in detail in the paragraphs to come).

Remember, though, that there is no hard and fast rule to non-linear speed reading. You, the speed reader, get to choose which parts of a text are important and which

If you don't retain and comprehend the reading material, your speed reading efforts are essentially rendered useless.

sections can be skimmed or passed over completely. Skim the "nonessentials" and dedicate your time and attention to the core concepts and ideas. Writers often add extra information to expound on ideas and provide examples to ensure readers have comprehended a particular topic, idea, or concept. If the idea is already clear to you and you don't need a further exemplification of a concept, skim the explanatory portions. Just keep in mind that although your primary goal of speed reading is to read at an accelerated pace, you still want to retain the key information you read. If you don't retain and comprehend the reading material, your speed reading efforts are essentially rendered useless.

Risks of Speed Reading

As you begin to dedicate your time to applying these methods, it's important to keep in mind one of the potential risks of speed reading—loss of comprehension. We introduced this topic back in Chapter 3 when we discussed the effectiveness of speed reading and what factors make for an effective and successful speed reader. If you've forgotten some of these points, we recommend going back to view them, but for your convenience, we've included a few points below.

1.) Speed reading works especially well if you:

- Have read the text beforehand and at least somewhat understood it

- Are looking for a particular passage

- Are using bullet points, bolded, italicized, or underlined words or phrases to gain a brief overview of the topic

- Are familiar with the topic

- Have read other materials that relate to the text.

2.) Some factors that affect our ability to speed reading include:

- The nature of the material (if it's a chapter book, academic writing, or full of technical words)

- Your alertness and ability to concentrate

- Your cognitive abilities and mental speed (a college graduate will be more successful than an elementary student)

- Amount of practice

Now, this doesn't mean that every time you speed read you'll miss a certain amount of vital information. Comprehension, as you can see from these above points, depends on the individual. What seems to be more universal among speed readers, however, is that comprehension tends to decline when we speed read larger volumes of text. As words accumulate, our brains require longer periods of time to process them. And because words are coming in at such a rapid pace when we speed read, the brain simply can't process all of the words at the same time—words sometimes come in faster than our brain is capable of registering and interpreting them.

The quick fix: Our brains sometimes struggle to maintain comprehension rates when we bombard them with large volumes of words at a rapid pace. If you feel like this happens to you, rest assured. Taking frequent short breaks as you read will give your brain the time it needs to absorb the information you've quickly loaded into it.

Additional tips

Be sure to avoid highlighting. Many people believe that using a highlighter will improve their reading speed and comprehension, but in all actuality, the reverse is true. Sometimes we highlight because we don't want to bother learning the material now, but we know it's important. You'll eventually end up reading the material twice, and that's certainly not helpful when you're speed reading.

Chapter 6—Preparing your Speed Reading

Environment

We've gone over three essential speed reading techniques in Chapter 4, as well as habits to avoid and be wary of as you speed read in Chapter 5. But before you actually sit down to apply these techniques as you speed read, you need to create a conducive and efficient speed reading environment for yourself.

So, what exactly makes a good speed reading environment?

Setting up an environment that promotes successful and focused speed reading is both a simple and complex task. We say this because there are both quick and long-term ways to ensure your concentration while speed reading. Some of these **quick methods** include:

- Eliminating technological distractions

- Making sure there is proper lighting

- ·Using reading glasses, if necessary

- Limiting your movement

- Maintaining a straight posture

One of the most productive **long-term strategies** you can use to create an efficient speed reading environment is:

- Reducing or eliminating sub-vocalization (quieting our mental voice as we read)

Quick ways to improve your speed reading environment

As you can hopefully see from the list above, there's a plethora of simple yet effective ways in which we can create or improve our speed reading environment. Most are pretty self-explanatory, but in case you're unsure about a few, or if you simply want to read about some suggestions, take a look at the following section that includes brief but helpful descriptions and suggestions about each quick method.

Eliminating technological distractions

Take a second to count how many electronic devices you have within arm's reach of at you this very moment. How many devices were you able to count? 1? 2? 3? 4+? If you don't have a cell phone and you're reading this book in paper-back form, you might be the exception. But more likely than not, you're reading this on a computer, tablet, or cell phone, and moreover, you probably have an additional device close by. Now, how many times do you think you've checked or used your phone since you began reading this? The answers may vary, but, for most people, it's probably been multiple times. What we're trying to show here is that we're surrounded by distracting technology, whether it's our cell phone, computer, tablet, television, or iPod.

So when you're trying to read a book, for example, at an unnaturally fast pace while simultaneously trying to comprehend and retain the information presented, checking your phone when it vibrates clearly won't be conducive to your reading process. You might lose your place in the book, forget what is being discussed, or accidentally read something you've just read. This is why it's important to switch your phones to silent, close your laptop (unless you're using it to read), and turn off any television programs.

Proper lighting

The quality of your light when you read is often an unacknowledged factor, but it's certainly not an irrelevant one. Poor lighting can lead to eye strain, which reduces your eyes' full potential to read quickly and efficiently. However, don't overcompensate with light, either. Bright lights tend to be distracting and the glare of bright lights can overwhelm the eyes and require more time for adjusting. You should also avoid reading under incandescent lights—these can lead to poor visual acuity and slow down reading rates as well.

Using your reading glasses

If you have reading glasses, use them. Not using them can reduce your visual sharpness and hinder your ability to see words instantly and clearly. If you find that you're squinting at words as you read them at either normal or accelerated speeds, you should consider going to your local optometrist (eye doctor) or purchasing an over-the-counter pair of reading glasses. While you'll likely need insurance to obtain reading glasses through your optometrist's office, over-the-counter reading glasses will cost on average of $2-5, depending on the store and location.

Limiting your movement

Most of us have those little annoying habits or movements that we do every so often. Some of us pick our nails and twirl our hair while others bit their lip and crack their knuckles. Whatever your guilty habit may be, it's important that you refrain from doing it as you speed read. Even if cracking your knuckles, for example, seems like a natural motion, your brain is still actively working and processing the movement as you do it. And when your brain is focusing on your hand movement, it's unable to dedicate its full attention to the words it's trying to read and comprehend. Therefore, it's important that you sit as still as possible. If you have a habit of doing something with your hands when you're concentrating, try placing them palm-down in your lap. Or, if you find that you move your feet around when you read, be sure to place them flat on the floor—and keep them there. These little things may not seem like a lot, but they absolutely do affect our concentration, and therefore, our ability to interpret, comprehend, and retain the words, sentences, and concepts that we encounter as we read.

Posture

When we say posture, we're talking about two things: your physical position as you read and the position of your reading material. So, as you prepare to speed read:

- **Sit in a comfortable position**, but try to make the upper half of your body as erect as possible. Keeping your shoulders back and your spine straight will help keep you alert and will prevent you from feeling tired as you read.

- **Place the text on a flat, sloped surface**. This slope should be angled toward your face rather than the ceiling. So, let's say that the slope should be at a 45 degree angle. Having the reading material set up this way will prevent you from having to bow your head or stoop your shoulders to see the text. Your surface should also be able to hold the reading material without you physically having to do so. When you don't need to hold the text, you won't be tempted to fidget with it or bend the corners of the pages— a constantly moving reading material is a major distraction, even to the most practiced speed reader because it forces us to focus and refocus our vision.

- **Place the text about 15 to 18 inches from your eyes.** Having it too close or too far will strain your eyes, which you absolutely want to avoid.

A long-term way to improve your reading environment: Sub-vocalization

Remember way back in Chapter 1 when we discussed how we mentally "hear" the words we read, even if we're not reading them aloud? Not sure what we mean? Pay attention to what you're doing right now as you read these very words. You're probably reading them in your head, right? You're probably not moving your mouth as you read them, too, correct? Do you notice how you still seem to hear these words as you read them, even when you read them in your head without moving your mouth? This is what we mean by "hearing" the words as we read them. This spontaneous and almost instinctual habit of mentally pronouncing or speaking the words that are being read is called **sub-vocalization.** It's a habit we all develop during the moments when we first learn to read.

We often think of our environment as being our physical location. We also tend to associate our environment as being made up of physical things and people. Interestingly however, we also have a mental environment. This mental environment is where sub-vocalization occurs. However, sub-vocalization is a habit we need to break, mainly because it makes the process of reading a text slower. While it certainly isn't improper (first-time readers benefit greatly from this technique), sub-vocalization takes up a lot of time. It also requires multiple organs to work simultaneously (our eyes, mouth, ears, and brain), which increases our fatigue. Here's a brief breakdown of what each organ is doing as you mentally sound out words:

- **Eyes:** As you read, the part of your eye called the retina transforms the images you see into electrical impulses that are carried through a nerve to your brain for interpretation.

- **Mouth:** Although sub-vocalization is a mental process, some people tend to silently mouth the words they read. When they do this, they stimulate the motor area of the brain that governs the movement of the tongue, lips, and other muscles involved in the motor process of speech.

- **Ears:** Even if you're not speaking words aloud as you read, your ears still tune in to what you're hearing in your mind. This means that the auditory part of your brain is stimulated and processing information.

- **Brain:** Your brain is highly stimulated and active as it assimilates and comprehends the signals it receives from your eyes (from looking at the words), your ears (from hearing the words mentally), and from your mouth (if you silently mouth words as you read).

For many of us, reading seems like a fairly simple process. Inside our bodies, however, multiple organs are constantly sending and receiving information from other organs. It's a complex and highly active series of processes that can result in fatigue, and will eventually lead to a decline in concentration and the ability to read and comprehend effectively.

So, you now know just how active our bodies are when we sub-vocalize. That's why it's important that we reduce our sub-vocalization as we read. However, reducing our tendency to sub-vocalize as we read is easier said than done. Like we've explained, it's an almost instinctual habit that we developed when we first began to read, which means it can be quite a trying task to eliminate our tendency to sub-vocalize. The good news is, though, that it can be done with great patience and even greater practice.

Techniques to limit sub-vocalization

In order to improve our speed reading rates, we need to quiet our mind by overriding or preventing sub-vocalization. Although it's a difficult, strange, and perhaps even uncomfortable learning process at first, eliminating our tendency to sub-vocalize is most widely done by very easy-to-do techniques.

Chew Gum

The simplest yet most effective and widely used technique to limit sub-vocalization is to chew gum as you speed read. When you chew gum, you give your mouth something else to do besides mentally vocalize or mouth the words you read. Just like you can't talk while chewing gum, your mouth can't interact with your brain. This is because when your mouth is preoccupied, the speech mechanisms in our brain are disengaged from the rest of the reading process. This is vital because this means the visual cortex of our brain can work and interpret the words we see without having to compete with other speech-related parts of the brain. And when our visual cortex takes over the reading process, the auditory part of our brain no longer has to expel energy on figuring out how to read and pronounce each word we come across as we speed read.

Hum

A similar logic as chewing gum rests behind humming as you speed read. Using the vocal cords in your throat will prevent your brain from mentally pronouncing each word you see.

Silencing your mind as you read by chewing gum or humming are just two of the many steps you can take to create a conducive speed reading environment. When speed readers combine these sub-vocalization-preventing techniques with the quick methods discussed earlier in the chapter, some have found that they were able to triple their starting reading speed. For many of those who were able to successfully do this, they were reading about 600-1200 words per minute.

Chapter 7—How to Practice Speed Reading

There's only one more topic that you need to familiarize yourself with and understand before you dive into speed reading. We promise. It's also a crucial one. Learning how to actually practice your speed reading is vital to your success because it requires time and dedication. The more practice you put into speed reading, the better results you'll see.

No matter your speed reading experience or success, this chapter will benefit *you*. The previous chapters that introduce techniques

The key to speed reading is to *slowly* apply new techniques and casually gain new awareness for your reading habits.

and habits to avoid while reading have been dedicated to beginner speed readers. However, we wanted to make sure that even an experienced speed reader would find and take something helpful and meaningful away from this book. Because of this, we've divided this chapter into three sections, each pertaining to different speed reading level. The first section is for the beginner speed reader who is just starting to speed read. The second section is dedicated to the intermediate speed reader, the reader who has some experience with speed reading but is still getting comfortable with it. The third section is for the expert speed reader who is looking to challenge himself or herself with more complicated passages or to refine their speed reading skills.

Speed reading for beginners

When you're first starting to apply the reading techniques as you speed read, it's highly recommended that you:

- **Select a non-fiction text:** Non-fiction reading materials tend to be based upon facts or reality, which makes it easier for you when you practice skim chunking or grouping noteworthy facts or ideas. Non-fiction ideas are often presented in a clear, concise, and organized way, compared to fictional works which often contain complex plots, intricate themes, and dynamic characters. Reading a text that you deem accessible is vital as you practice applying your speed reading technique while you read.

- **Read materials with large print:** A text with large print is ideal for speed reading practice—you won't require your eyes to work as hard as they would reading small print, and you should reduce the frequency of which you lose your place in the text.

- **Choose something without pictures:** Although pictures are helpful in reaffirming something you've just read or clarifying an explanation that was confusing, they can be a source of distraction for the beginning speed reader. You'll probably find that your eyes are naturally attracted to the colorful images or bold bar graphs provided in a text—ignore them. Better yet, avoid them.

- **Find a topic that is light and interesting to *you*:** Speed reading will generally go a lot smoother if you're interesting in the material. A topic that interests you will increase concentrate and promote comprehension.

When you're beginning to speed read a text that meets the above criteria, be sure to:

- **Trace your fingertip underneath the text line:** Use your finger or a pen as a tracker and pacer for your eyes. You want to get your eyes comfortable with moving at a faster pace, but don't worry about comprehending the material you read, at least at this point in time. Start by positioning either your right or left hand index finger by the left hand margin of the page, about ¾ of an inch from the edge. Move your fingertip toward the right hand margin until you're about ¾ of an inch from the right edge (The ¾ of an inch space before both margins prevents your eyes from resting on half-empty space.) As you keep it below the text line currently being read, be sure to move your finger at an even and steady pace. Your finger should serve as a pacer as it attracts your eyes' attention as you scan the text.

- **Test out chunking and your peripheral vision:** You won't know what speed reading techniques work best for you until you try them. You might feel very comfortable skim chunking and diagonal chunking, for example, but perhaps you simply don't like reading with your peripheral vision. Although using the combination of all of these techniques is highly recommended, it's not required. If using your peripheral vision slows your reading process down, don't use it. Find what works best for you and practice it each time you sit down to read.

- **Practice speed reading for at least 15 minutes each day:** Speed reading is a skill that requires dedication, patience, and time—a lot of it, oftentimes. To get the most out of your time, be sure to practice during early mornings after you've eaten breakfast. Experts suggest that we learn the best and are the most productive during this time of day. Most importantly, remember that the more often you practice, the better you will become. Speed reading becomes more natural when we make it a part of our everyday reading experience.

Things to keep in mind as you practice:

Note that speed reading is not applicable for every reading material. Texts that are detail-specific in nature such as legal documents, annual reports, instructions, and other legal or business-related materials should be read in the traditional word-by-word approach to ensure that you've comprehended the material and that crucial information hasn't been accidently overlooked. Personal letters, too, should be read normally. Applying speed reading techniques to personal letters oftentimes strips the notes of their emotions and meanings.

Speed reading for intermediates

If you've spent some time practicing and are starting to feel comfortable with the application of speed reading techniques, then you're probably an intermediary-level speed reader. At this point you should feel somewhat comfortable with chunking, using peripheral vision, limiting regression, avoiding linear reading, and creating an environment that is free of potential distractions. If you've practiced speed reading with picture-less texts with large font, we recommend that you now:

- **Choose cross-genre reading material:** Intermediate speed readers are welcome to choose from any type of genre they want (Fiction, non-fiction, biography, autobiography, poetry, fantasy, historical fiction, etc.) You should feel comfortable speeding reading through more creative materials that may not follow the standards of written language—poetry might employ slang words that you don't often confront in your everyday life, fantasy novels might submerge you in a world that is complicated and unlike your own, and fictional works might contain tangled plots and complex characters.

- **Select text with medium size font:** Because you're getting the hang of speed reading, you can now put a little more strain on your eyes, if need be, by reading smaller fonts. Chunking should be starting to feel like a natural reading process, so you can allow your eyes to do a little more work as they focus and refocus on your reading material's font. Of course, reading material with larger font is always best for speed readers. But, keep in mind that practicing reading on smaller font will only make your job easier when you speed read a text with larger font.

- **Read about a topic that you're unfamiliar with:** Speed reading becomes more complicated when we confront a text that we are unfamiliar with or when we encounter reading material that uses words we don't understand. Forcing yourself into these challenging positions will teach you how to overcome them and will help you determine which reading techniques work best for you when you're in such positions.

When you've chosen the genre, font size, and topic of your text, and you're ready to sit down and practice speed reading the material, remember to:

- **Use a pen to pace your eyes while comprehending the material:** As a beginner, it's recommended that you get comfortable using your fingertip to track and pace your eyes, but it's not required that you comprehend the material as you do so. As an intermediate speed reader, however, it is. (If you've forgotten how to effectively use a pacer as you speed read, refer to the above section called "Speed reading for beginners."

- **Use whatever speed reading technique you've discovered works best for you:** This can be skim chunking, diagonal chunking, using peripheral vision, or a combination of two or all three. By this point you should know what methods work best for you, and moreover, be comfortable with applying them as you read.

- **Be conscious of regression and linear reading:** Now that you're starting to feel comfortable with applying chunking and peripheral vision as you read, you should also start to take note of whether or not you have the tendency to reread material and read linearly. The key to speed reading is to *slowly* apply new techniques and gain new awareness for your reading habits.

- **Take note of any distractions:** As you practice speed reading, try to take note of anything that might be distracting you. Is the sound of your clock ticking across the room distracting you in even the slightest way? If so, remove it. Sometimes creating an environment conducive to efficient and successful speed reading is an ongoing process.

Speed reading for experts

At this point, you should be a confident and efficient speed reader. You should know what combination of speed reading techniques work best for you, should have eliminated the bad habits of regression and linear reading from your reading process, and should have successfully established a productive reading environment. You should have noticed a considerable increase in the amount of words you can read per minute. At this point, there are not many new things you can practice except for reading more complicated and challenging materials. This simple step can show drastic and lasting results, however, so don't feel like you've hit a dead end. When you practice, be sure to read:

- **Texts with topics that are unfamiliar or complex:** Reading materials that contain discussions about topics that are complex in nature will naturally be hard to retain information from and comprehend. Your lack of background knowledge will make you feel like you need to speed more time with the material—try to limit this urge. Instead, continue to speed read and retain only the most vital pieces of information. Practicing this will make speed reading less complicated materials seem like a breeze.

- **Reading material riddled with technical or unknown words:** When we come across words we don't know, we have the tendency to pause. Because you're an expert speed reader, you need to strengthen your ability to not be phased by the frequent encounter of words you don't know.

- **Texts with small print and pictures:** Texts with small print and pictures will truly test your abilities as a speed reader. The small text will eventually put a strain on your eyes and result in loss of comprehension. Your job is to work through this strain and retain as much vital information as you possibly can. Although you should be taking occasional breaks as you speed read, working through the exhaustion should help build your mental strength and endurance. Pictures, too, will affect comprehension. They have the ability to steal your attention from the text—don't let this happen. Fighting the urge to look at pictures when you already understand the text can help improve concentration skills and will make maintaining concentration when you read less complicated texts so much easier.

Chapter 8—Speed Reading Practice

Check-in point: Summary

We've gone over *a lot* of crucial speed reading information so far. As you're progressing through this book and preparing to apply several speed reading techniques as you read, it's important to recall all that you've learned. To make this process go smoother, we've included a brief summary of the techniques we've discussed so far.

Speed reading techniques:

- **Skim chunking:** While you quickly read through the text, remember certain groups of words or phrases that, when taken out of context, still give you a solid idea of what the reading material was about

- **Diagonal chunking:** Move your eyes in a Z-like fashion as you speed read a text. Start by reading the first sentence in full, then read the first 2-3 words of the left side of the second line of text and the last 2-3 words of the right side of the second line of text. Then read the first 2-3 words of the left side of the third line and the last 2-3 words of the right side of the third line. Continue this reading pattern as you work through the text.

- **Using your peripheral vision:** When we take advantage of our ability to see 180 degrees, we can generally read 4-5 words at a time. Relax your gaze and focus on expanding your sight so that you can take in multiple words at a time instead of focusing on one single word in your line of vision.

Habits to avoid:

- **Regression:** Don't read material you've already read. Maintaining your concentration by limiting distractions around you will help prevent this.

- **Linear Reading:** Don't feel obligated to read each and every word you see on a page. Likewise, don't feel like you must always read every sentence from left to right. If you have an understanding of the material, look for bolded, italicized, underlined, bulleted, or asterisked words, phrases, or sentences. These will usually indicate an important term or concept that is crucial for your understanding. Jumping around will help you cover more material in less time.

- **Sub-vocalization:** The habit of mentally sounding out words as we read causes our eyes, ears, mouth, and brain to tire out faster, which will result in your decreased concentration and comprehension. Chew gum or hum to help yourself avoid doing this instinctual reading habit.

Creating your reading environment:

- Reduce distractions

- Improve lighting

- Wear glasses, if need be

- Limit movement

- Sit straight and position your text at a 45 degree slope 18 inches from your face

Your turn: Speed reading exercises

Like we said, this chapter is dedicated to helping speed readers of all levels. So with that in mind, we've included 3 different reading exercises that are directed toward each speed reading fluency: beginner, intermediary, and expert. Decide what level you are and try the appropriate exercise. But remember, be honest with yourself. Attempting to read the text designed for an expert when you're just beginning to practice your speed reading skill will not help you—it might actually be counterproductive. Determine what you feel *comfortable* doing. If you have some experience with speed reading but find that the intermediary reading material is too difficult or frustrating, try the beginner text. Don't feel bad if this happens. Speed reading is a hard skill that nearly everyone struggles to master.

Speed reading exercise for <u>Beginners</u>

Directions: Time yourself. As you read the following text, you should begin to use the speed reading techniques of skim chunking, diagonal chunking, and peripheral vision. Trace the tip of a pen below the text as you read to ensure that your eyes are constantly moving forward. When you finish, complete the accessment questions following the text.

Mat Johnson is a twenty-first-century American author of literary fiction and graphic novels. He was born on August 19, 1970 and raised in Philadelphia by his African American mother. He attended Greene Street Friends School, West Chester University, University of Wales, Swansea, and eventually earned his B.A from Earlham College and recieved his M.F.A from Columbia University School of Arts. In addition to his many years of schooling, Johnson was awarded and named the first USA James Baldwin fellow by the United States Artist Foundation, a fellowship that grants inidividual artists an unrestricted $50,000 monetary award and the recognition of being one of America's most accomplished, creative, and innovative artists. Johnson's success after being named this reicipient would not stop there, however.

Aside from his academic success, Johnson has also achieved great success as a contemporary American author. His noteable prose works include his novels *Pym* and *Incognegro,* both of which are overwhelming about race and racism. *Pym,* published in 2011, is a spin-off novel of canonical author Edgar Allan Poe's *The Narrative of Arthur Gordon Pym of Nantucket* (1838). But while Poe's novel carries with it an often serious and heavy tone, Johnson's *Pym* approaches *Arthur Gordon Pym*'s racist conceptions with a biting satire that readers can't help but laught at and appreciate. At the same time, however, Johnson's novel does critically address the racism that Poe's novel displays.

His other novel, *Incognegro,* is a black-and-white graphic novel first published in February 2008 by DC Comics imprint Vertigo. It follows black protagonist Zane Pinchback as he investigates lynchings as an undercover white reporter for a black New York City newspaper. Things become complicated for Pinchback, however, when his brother is convicted of murder just before Pinchback plans to retire. Like *Pym, Incognegro* is largely interested in highlighting the racist mindsets of society and providing critical racial commentary on our conceptions of race and racial passing.

Although he is generally best known for *Pym* and *Incognegro,* Johnson has also published a varity of other works spanning across the genres of fiction, non-fiction, graphic novels, and anthologies. *Drop* (2000), *Hunting in Harlem* (2003), *Loving Day* (2015), *The Great Negro Plot* (2007), *Hellblazer* (2005), and *Black Cool: One Thousand Streams of Blackness* (2012) are just a few to note. What's interesting about many of these titles are their reference to race, which makes sense considering Johnson's own race and his upbringing in what he claims was a stratisfied neighrborhood.

Your Assessment

It's one thing to practice speed reading. It's another thing to practice and reflect on your experience. This is what we're asking you to do here. For you to improve your words per minute rate and increase your comprehension, you first need to know in what areas you excel at and in what areas you need to further practice, improve, and refine. With that in mind, answer:

- How many seconds/minutes did it take you to read the above text? _____seconds/ minutes.
- How many words were you able to read per minute? _____wpm.
  - To figure this out, you will need to divided the total number of words from the above text (407) by the amount of time it took you to read the text.

Without looking back at the passage, answer the following questions, either mentally or by writing them down.

- Who is the passage about?
- What was his/her childhood/upbringing like?
- What is his/her career?
- What awards has he/she recieved?
- What is he/she best known for?
- The passage discusses 2 particular works. What are they called?
- How are these two works similar? How are they different?
- What genres does this person write in?
- Make an inference: What seems to be a common theme among his/her works? Why might this be?

If you were able to answer <u>all or most of these question,</u> consider:

How long did you spend reading the text?

- If it took you more than a minute and a half, you spent too long reading.
- If it took you less than a minute to read the text, you successfully sped read *and* comprehended the material. Well done.

If you were not able to answer at least half of these questions, consider:

How long did you spend reading the text?

- If it took you less than 30 seconds and you did not comprehend the material, you may want to speed just a little more time reading. Remember, speed reading is a useless skill unless you are able to retain and remember the information you've read.

- If it took you more than a minute and a half to read the text and you did not comprehend at least half of the material, try:
  - Reviewing the skim chunking, diagonal chunking, and peripheral vision techniques we discussed earlier and reapply them next time you read.
  - Briefly glancing over the text before you speed read it.
  - Observing your environment—are there distractions? Is it well light? Are you in a comfortable but upright position with the material at a 45 degree slope?

Reflect upon and answer the following questions as honestly as you can:

1. What areas of this text did you **struggle** with, if any? (Did technical words slow you down? Did you find the literary conversation to be confusing?)

2. What areas of this text did you **excel** at, if any? (Have you read about Mat Johnson's biography before? Are you famailiar with either or both of his works?)

3. What **techniques** did you use while speed reading, if any?

- Of the techinques you applied, which ones worked best?

- If you used skim chunking, which words did you group?

- Would you use the technique(s) you applied again?

4. How do you think you could **improve** your speed reading next time?

If you've completed this exercise, answered the following assessment and reflection questions, but still find that you're having trouble speed reading after reviewing the earlier material and practicing, don't get discouraged. Speed reading is an unnatural skill that involves us breaking all of the reading habits we've been practicing since a very early age. The best thing you can do is to keep practicing and reviewing the reading techniques.

Speed reading exercise for <u>Intermediates</u>

Directions: *Time yourself. As you read the following text, you should apply the speed reading techinques that work best for you. You should also begin taking note of whether or not you find yourself regressing or reading linearly. Continue to use a pacer as you skim the text. When you finish, complete the accessment questions following the text.*

The development of the American atomic bomb carried with it a multitude of moral and ethical dilemmas, which led to controversial debates regarding both its research and development. Yet the decision to drop the bomb also sparked countless scholarly works that reflected the concerns and ideas surrounding the deployment of the bomb on Japan. While many historians have asserted their belief that the United States dropped the bomb to shorten the war and reduce the amount of American casualties, others argued and provided thought-provoking evidence that suggested that the United States' decision to drop the bomb revolved around ulterior motives. Those who asserted such statements drew upon historical documents such as President Truman's memoirs and Henry L. Stimson's writings, which highlighted the idea that using the atomic bombs on Japan would shorten the duration of the war and save American lives. However, the same documents also portrayed the United States' concern over Russia's desire to further expand its influence and control in the Far East. Moreover, through the works of Truman and Stimson, it is suggested that the United States dropped the atomic bomb on Japan not only to shorten the war and save lives, but also as a tool to intimidate Russia and control Stalin's expansionist progressions in Eastern Europe.

Among many of the documents that circulated after the events in Hiroshima and Nagasaki was Henry L. Stimson's "The Decision to Use the Atomic Bomb," an article in which Stimson expressed the factors that led to the United States' decision to drop the atomic bomb. Describing the initial reasons for the United States' pursuance of the bomb's production, Stimson wrote, "The original experimental achievement of atomic fission had occurred in Germany in 1938, and it was known that the Germans had continued their experiments. In 1941 and 1942 they were believed to be ahead of us, and it was vital that they should not be the first to bring atomic weapons into the field of battle." Like Stimson, most scientists justified the bomb project on the grounds that the United States' possession of an atomic bomb would act as a deterrent against Germany. "Furthermore," Stimson continued, "if we should be the first to develop the weapon, we should have a great new instrument for shortening the war and minimizing destruction." Stimson not only viewed the bomb as a deterrent against Germany, but also as a tool that would shorten the war and limit the number of American casualties. To further justify the decision to use the bomb, Stimson recorded estimates of when the war would be likely to end and how many casualties would be expected, should the United States follow through with their planned land invasion in Japan. On this he wrote, "We estimated that if we should be forced to carry this plan to its conclusion, the major fighting would not end until the later part of 1946, at the earliest. I was informed that such operations might be expected to cost over a million casualties, to American forces alone." However, this estimate was troublesome, as Stimson made no reference to where this information came from. Did he hear this in a meeting, or was this simply his own calculations?

Similar to Stimson, President Harry S. Truman's *Memoirs of Harry S. Truman* conveyed the reasoning behind dropping the bomb, along with the projected death estimates that would result from the United States' land invasion of Japan. In his memoirs, Truman stated, "We could hope for a miracle, but the daily tragedy of a bitter war crowded in on us. We labored to construct a weapon of such overpowering force that the enemy could be forced to yield swiftly once we could resort to it. This was the primary aim of our secret and vast effort." Truman's explanation that the bomb would cause Japan to "swiftly yield" suggested his agreement with Stimson that the atomic bomb would indeed shorten the war in the Pacific. Although both Stimson and Truman agreed upon the bomb's ability to shorten the war, Truman's estimates on American casualties differed drastically from Stimson's. Compared to Stimson's estimated one million casualties, Truman proposed, based on General Marshall's calculations, that the physical conquest of Japan would "cost half a million American lives to force the enemy's surrender on his home grounds." Truman referenced the source of his information as Marshall, yet it remained unclear where Marshall was receiving his information. Furthermore, the drastically different estimates between Stimson and Truman's accounts raised several questions among historians, relating to why neither war-time official was able to link their estimates to a credible source. Historians who argued that the United States had different motives to dropping the bomb would also argue that this disunity between estimated casualties reflected the United States' low importance set on casualty statistics, suggesting that their focus was instead on a different matter.

Your Assessment

- How many minutes did it take you to read the above text? _____ minutes.
- How many words were you able to read per minute? _____wpm.
    o To figure this out, you will need to divided the total number of words from the above text (808) by the amount of time it took you to read the text.

Without looking back at the passage, answer the following questions, either mentally or by writing them down.

- What historical event does this essay discuss?
- What is the main argument of the essay (What is its thesis?)
- What problems, if any, does the author suggest?
- What two primary text does this essay reference?
  - What is the main idea of the first source referenced?
  - What is the main idea of the second source referenced?
- Does the essay resolve the problem addressed?
- Reflect: Do you share the same opinions as the author?

1. What areas of this text did you **struggle** with, if any? (Do you know very little about this historical time period or event? Are you unfamailiar with the non-fiction genre?)

2. What areas of this text did you **excel** at, if any? (Are you a WWII history buff?)

3. What **techniques** did you use while speed reading, if any?

- Of the techinques you applied, which ones worked best?
- If you used skim chunking, which words did you group?
- Would you use the technique(s) you applied again?

4. How do you think you could **improve** your speed reading next time?

Speed reading exercise for <u>Experts</u>

Directions: Time yourself. Actively apply your reading techniques as you read the following material. When you finish, complete the following assement and reflection questions.

Jonathan Edwards' sermon is engaging, entertaining, and frightening, for the religiously devout, all at the same time. His writing is filled with terror-provoking images that capture a vengeful and wrathful God whose "mere pleasure" keeps "wicked men at any one moment out of hell" (431). And although "Sinners in the Hands of an Angry God" is filled with dark ideas, vivid imagery, and terrifying metaphors, it is important to note the way Edwards goes about explaining and describing these devices, which is based almost entirely upon tactile perception, the sense of touch. His approach is in contrast with Puritan sermon writer Thomas Hooker, and through a comparison of both texts, it becomes clear that Edwards' writing is exceptional and innovative. On the surface, his sermon is simple, but it brings forth many unparalleled concepts, begging the reader to ask: why does Edwards describe such a violent God? Does intensifying the sense of touch and excluding all other senses serve a purpose? If so, what is that purpose? Moreover, analysis of Edwards' sermon in regards to the focus on tactile perception, particularly the sense of touch and the obscuring of the other four senses, highlights a new approach to the sermon, which works to catch the Puritan listener's attention through a relatable, aggressive, and fear-instilling tactic.

At first it may seem strange to assert that Edwards focuses solely upon tactile perception, but once the text is read through this lens, it becomes quite clear that Edwards does this almost relentlessly. In fact, it is impossible to read his text without being bombarded with physically vivid and intense descriptions of touch. Thomas J. Steele and Eugene Delay write in their essay "Vertigo in History: The Threatening Tactility of 'Sinners in the Hands'" that Edwards' writing is "truly 'sensational' preaching" (242). The notion that Edwards uses a strictly sensational sermon is supported within the text, seen through the reader's ability to flip to any page of "Sinners in the Hands of an Angry God" and find imagery of "fiery floods of...fierceness" with "inconceivable fury," (435) actions that will "inflict wrath without any pity," (437) and diction that suggests God will "tread" upon, "trample," and "crush" Puritan sinners (438). Edwards is working toward a new approach to the sermon through his use of violently physical imagery, metaphor, and diction. In response to this idea, Edwin H. Cady, author of "The Artistry of Jonathan Edwards," suggests that Puritan audiences were becoming immune to even the most powerful sermons, which prompted Edwards' tactic of fear-instilling aggressiveness. Cady writes, "Enfield must have heard [sermons] from the same pulpit many times before; and they must have slipped through the minds of Edwards' hearers like water-worn pebbles, not arousing sensation or stimulating reaction" (64). Cady's assertion that Puritan audiences were losing interest would likely have motivated Edwards' aggressive preaching style and approach, which focuses on wrathful and fierce physical sensations. But why does this focus on the sense of touch make Edwards' sermon so successful?

Edwards' "Sinners" sermon was delivered in Enfield, Connecticut, a small New England town, on July 8, 1741. During his sermon, Edwards captures the audience's attention by relating God's wrath to something the community is familiar with-water. This idea is seen as Edwards explains the intensity of God's wrath through this simile: "The wrath of God is like great waters that are dammed for the present; they increase more and more, and rise higher and higher, till an outlet is given; and the longer the stream is stopped, the more rapid and mighty is its course when once it is let loose" (435). This idea of uncontainable and damaging water directly relates to Enfield, and moreover, a powerful, consuming, and uncontrollable rush of water was a common threat to the community. Cady expounds on this idea, explaining in regards to Enfield that, "The dramatic peril of floods as well as the daily power of the falling waters were familiar and exciting. And Edwards took the stuff of his hearers' own minds, raised it to the plane of his own intensity, and made his vision live in those minds" (66). Cady asserts an excellent point here as he explains that Edwards applied the community's fear of water to his metaphors that describe God's wrath, making the metaphor much more personal. And to make matters worse, while negatively appealing to

New Englanders' anxieties, Edwards blames the threat of a vehement burst of water on the omnipotent power of God. Edwards captures the sensation of uncontrolled water as he writes, "and if your strength were ten thousand times greater than it is, yea, ten thousand time greater than the strength of the stoutest, sturdiest devil in hell, it would be nothing to withstand or endure it" (435). Here Edwards explains that even superior, supernatural strength will not save the Puritan community from either rushing water or God's forceful wrath. Moreover, through the cultural context in which "Sinners" is preached, we begin to see cultural inflows which aid in understanding why Edwards' sermon, through the lens of tactile perception, was highly successful and powerful compared to others Puritan sermons- he focuses on the fear of his audience.

The sensation of physical touch is present throughout Edwards' sermon, but the other four senses, interestingly, are skewed. Edwards includes the senses, sight and sound in particular, but he manipulates them. He repeats that it is "only the power and mere pleasure of God that holds you up" from the flames of hell, but he never truly describes those flames (434). What color are the flames of hell? Are the flames a thin wisps of fire? Are they a raging tornado of heat? Both the audience and the reader are left wondering this because unlike his imagery for tactile perception, a visual description for sight is omitted. Edwards describes, "There is the dreadful pit of the glowing flames of the wrath of God; there is hell's wide gaping mouth open" (434).

The only image Edwards supplies the reader with is images of glowing flames and hell's "gaping mouth" (434). Furthermore, after reading his sermon, it becomes clear to the reader that this is an unnaturally mild description for Edwards. On this topic, Cady writes, "pictures of hell-fire appear to be neither its most vivid nor its most numerous images...Edwards made surprisingly little effort to actualize fire for his audience. He used no color words and no objective heat words" (69). Cady too questions Edwards' lack of imagery for sight. But for someone who has such an art for manipulating and terrifying his audience, there must be a reason for omitting the sense of sight. Perhaps Edwards skims over visual descriptions because it allows his audience to create their own personal, terrifying ideas of hell, thus making proper use of the imagination. Through the absence of description, each audience member will envision their worst nightmare. And because not everyone has the same fears and weaknesses, Edwards' lack of visual imagery makes it so that no one person views hell any less horrible than the other, so that no one is excluded from this atrocious experience. After all, a God who "will have no compassion upon you" and who will "have no regard to your welfare" will not hesitate in creating the most dreadful, miserable, torturous place to exist (437).

Your Assessment

- How many minutes did it take you to read the above text? _____ minutes.
- How many words were you able to read per minute? _____wpm.

- o To figure this out, you will need to divided the total number of words from the above text (1,216) by the amount of time it took you to read the text.

Without looking back at the passage, answer the following questions, either mentally or by writing them down.

- What author is this text about and which work of his does this essay explore?
- What is this essay about?
- What specific sense does this essay explore in the author's work?
- According to Cady, what was the author's motivation behind his work?
- How does the author discussed in the essay capture his audience's attention?
- What senses are ignored in the work discussed in this essay?

Reflect upon and answer the following questions as honestly as you can:

1. What areas of this text did you **struggle** with, if any? (Did technical words slow you down? Did you find the literary conversation to be confusing?)

2. What areas of this text did you **excel** at, if any? (Have you read Jonathan Edward's sermons before? Are you at all famailiar with the Puritans and their literary history?)

3. What **techniques** did you use while speed reading, if any?

- Of the techinques you applied, which ones worked best?
- If you used skim chunking, which words did you group?
- Would you use the technique(s) you applied again?

4. How do you think you could **improve** your speed reading next time?

Chapter 9—Speed Skimming "How to" Books

Even when you weren't familiar with speed reading techniques, you probably skimmed a text at one point. You most likely have read multiple lines of text without necessarily focusing on each word, its meaning, and its significance, right? Well, speed skimming is just an accelerated version of skimming.

Speed Skimming Myth: You must read every word in a non-fiction book.

Skimming: Casually but quickly reading a text to find its main ideas and supporting details.

Speed Skimming: Quickly reading a text to get a general gist of its main ideas.

When should I speed skim?

We oftentimes speed read when we want to learn, retain, and comprehend a large amount of information in a short amount of time. Speed skimming is a bit different because we speed skim when we generally want to get the gist of something without bombarding ourselves with all the details. So, you should speed skim when:

- You want to understand just the main idea or argument without reading all the words

- You want to learn the basics of the topic without all the details or examples

- You've read the text before and are looking for a particular passage

What should I speed skim?

You can essentially speed skim any material that has writing. However, there are certain genres that speed skimming produces better results for. Novels, for example, aren't the best reading materials to speed skim if you're reading them for enjoyment. They are often constructed with complex plots and dynamic characters, which makes finding and pulling the main ideas a complicated process without a close examination. "Self-help" or "how-to" books, on the other hand, are oftentimes great reading materials to apply speed skimming to. This is because they are often structured around one main idea—either fixing a problem or learning a new skill.

How do I speed skim?

If you're feeling comfortable with the speed reading

process, speed skimming will be a breeze. It's far less complex than speed reading because it's not really about techniques. Instead, speed skimming is all about knowing what to read and where to find it. So next time you sit down to speed skim, try:

- **Speed skimming just the first sentence of a paragraph:** With the exception of a few reading materials such as novels, the first sentence of a paragraph should be the topic sentence, which typically give a generally sense of what the paragraph is about (its main ideas, concerns, or interests).

  When you read this first part of a sentence, you'll be able to tell if the rest is worth reading. If it is, slow

  Noteworthy fact: We can find 70-80% of the most important information of a 250 pages book within 15-60 minutes of speed skimming.

  down your skimming and spend a little more time reading. If it's not, simply move on to the next paragraph.

- **Speed skimming the first and last sentence of a paragraph:** If you have a little more time on your hands, try speed skimming both the first and last sentences of a paragraph. Like we just discussed, the first sentence usually tells you what the paragraph is about. The last sentence is also an important one for speed skimming, however. It usually gives some type of conclusion or wrap-up statement about the paragraph. This speed skimming technique is especially useful if you're reading an academic essay or article because academic writing is usually organized by introduction and conclusions—the first sentence will tell you the main idea of the paragraph and the last sentence will restate what has been discussed so far.

- **Speed skimming just the headers of a paragraph:** If you're in a rush, speed skimming the headers and subtitles of a text can be surprisingly helpful. For example, if you see a header titled "The Visual and Mechanical Process of Speed Reading," you'll be able to infer that that section of writing will most likely talk about what the visual cortex of your brain does as you speed read. If you're looking for information on speed reading techniques, however, this section won't be very helpful. But fortunately, speed skimming the header informed you of this before you actually read the material.

Speed Skimming Fact:

You can get necessary information without reading every single word or missing the main ideas. Search for "the golden nugget" of the text.

Speed skimming is a valuable technique for anyone who must read pages upon pages of writing a day, but isn't required to grasps hold of and retain all the little details of the text. Speed skimming is all about searching for the most important information in the book, the **"golden nugget"** of a text.

As you search for this golden nugget of information, it's important to keep in mind that not every single page of writing is golden—some pages will simply serve as a build up to the main ideas of a text and some will simply conclude by reviewing what's been discussed. <u>We must be gold miners</u> as we speed skim our reading materials. And for those who feel uncomfortable with or guilty of not reading a book in its entirety, don't! The author of the book already has your money. They won't be offended, we promise.

Chapter 10: Further Suggestions

You've dedicated a good portion of your time to learning about the most effective speed reading techniques and applying them to the speed reading exercises found in Chapter 8. But what now? Well, speed reading is all about practice and consistency, so it's highly recommended that you find activities or ways to make speed reading an active process in your life. If you're a bit unsure of how to proceed, we've included a few suggestions to help you out. You've hopefully learned so much from this book—we don't want you to lose any of it.

Recommended Courses

Sometimes practicing and refining your speed reading skills takes more than simply reading a book or two. Although Chapter 8 of this book did provide three different materials that you could practice your speed reading on (depending on your experience), you'll need to practice much more. Online speed reading courses are a great way to expand your knowledge and further practice your skills. But before we recommend some of the most popular and best reviewed online speed reading courses, you should have some idea of what to look for in a course. So, whether you follow through with our recommendations or choose to find your own course, make sure the course you enroll in offers:

- Teaching modules that both test your reading speed and offer ways to improve it

- Modules that let you progress at your own pace

- Programs that let you change the size of the page/text

- Exercises that test chunking techniques, peripheral vision, and comprehension

- An easy-to-use format

- Customer service and online help and support (in case you have trouble logging into your account)

The following courses we recommend meet these 6 above requirements and offer a plethora of additional and helpful services as well.

1. Rev It Up Reading: We love this online course because it comes with a free downloadable eBook and allows users to participate in an interactive class with the program's designer, Abby Marks Beale. The program's dedication to helping you learn to read quicker while simultaneously maintaining high comprehension rates makes it the ideal course for the beginner speed reader. The course will cost you about $200, but its innovative interface and flawless software will make it worth your while and money.

2. RocketReader: If you feel confident with speed reading techniques and are interested in finding a course that offers an extensive variety of unique speed reading exercises and tests, this is the course for you. It's the perfect course for the intermediate or expert speed reader who feels comfortable using their skills but is in search of ways to practice and refine their speed reading skills. Its online speed reading course isn't quite as clear as Rev it Up Reading's, but in return, it offers a free trial and the cost of the course is a bit cheaper, too—it'll run you about $140.

Conclusion

Speed reading is about creating a firm foundation and expanding off of it. It's about learning and mastering the techniques of speed reading, gaining awareness for you own reading habits, and learning to transform those hindering habits into practices conducive to reading at accelerated speeds. But most importantly, speed reading is all about practice. It's an unnatural skill for us to have, so naturally the development of speed reading skills can be a time-consuming process. Fortunately, the wide-array of techniques, tips, and suggestions mentioned throughout this book will help shave off some time from this process. Whether you decide to apply skim chunking, diagonal chunking, or using your peripheral vision as you read, you'll now be able to read and comprehend the most important sections of lengthy texts in a dramatically reduced amount of time. By gaining awareness for your habit of regressing, linearly reading, or sub-vocalizing, you're now on your way toward cutting these habits from your reading process and replacing them with ones conducive to your reading success. You've learned about creating a distraction-free environment that fosters good speed reading habits and have practiced your skills in that very environment, so now you're ready to branch off and try some highly recommended online speed reading courses.

If you take one thing from this book, it should be that speed reading requires practice. But with your dedication, patience, and motivation, learning and applying the techniques and suggestions we've discussed throughout this book will help you improve your reading rate and gain a confidence for speed reading within as little as 12 hours.

30051679R00062

Made in the USA
Middletown, DE
16 March 2016